Pam

KENT
COUNTRY RECIPES

COMPILED BY
ANN GOMAR

ℛℛ
Ravette London

Published by Ravette Limited,
3 Glenside Estate, Star Road,
Partridge Green, Horsham,
Sussex RH13 8RA.
(0403) 710392

Production - Oval Projects Ltd.
Cover design - Jim Wire
Typesetting - Repro-type
Printing & binding - Cox & Wyman Ltd.

Acknowledgements:
Grateful thanks are extended to the many people of Kent who have
contributed towards this collection of recipes, including:

Pearl L. Frewin of Faversham for Canterbury Puddings

Mrs. Rosemary Gitsham for Herb Pie

Clive & Rita Kingston of The Royal Hotel, Deal, for Seabass stuffed
with Crab Meat created especially for this book.

Colin Botley of The Shant Hotel, East Sutton, for Chicken in Hochee
and Shant Stewed Steak

Peggie Batty for Boiled Leg of Lamb in Caper Sauce and Rock Cakes

The Kent Archives Office for Hodge Podge and a number of other old
handwritten recipes

Alison Revell, Assistant Archivist, Kent, for Margate Ale from A
Kentish Cookery Collection.

The recipes contained in this book are traditional and many have been
compiled from archival sources. Every effort has been made to ensure
that the recipes are correct.

RECIPES

SOUPS and BEGINNINGS
Creamed Green Pea Soup 9
St. Margaret's Bay Prawns in Tomatoes 10
Creamy Shrimp Toasts 11
Twice Laid 12
Whitstable Oysters 12

FISH
Baked Rochester Smelts 13
Mussels in White Wine 14
Dover Sole in White Wine 15
Seaflower 16
Beer Batter 17

POULTRY and GAME
Pheasant in Port Wine 18
Kentish Chicken Pudding 19
Chicken in Hochee 20
Casserole of Rabbit with Red Wine 21

MEAT
Steak and Oyster Pudding 22
Shant Stewed Steak 23
Herb Pie 24
Beef in Beer 25
Hodge Podge 26
Boiled Leg of Lamb in Caper Sauce 27
Pork Chops in Beer 28
Pork and Apple Pie 29
Tonbridge Brawn 30
Faggots 31

VEGETABLES

Creamed Cabbage   32
Brussels Sprouts with Chestnuts   33
Kentish Cauliflower with Shrimp Sauce   34

CHEESE DISHES

Cauliflower Cheese from the Isle of Thanet   35
Kentish Rarebit   36
Kentish Cheese Pasties   36
Cheese and Apple Pie   37
Gran Gomar's Cheese Supper Dish   38
Cob Nut and Cheese Savoury Bake   39

PUDDINGS

Floating Island   40
New Year's Pudding   41
Kent Well Pudding   42
Rochester Syrup Pudding   43
Kentish Pudding Pie   44
Apple Pie   45
Sponge Hedgehog   46
Rhubarb Hedgehog   47
Little Canterbury Puddings with Gooseberries   48
Apple Charlotte   49
Apple Fritters with Beer   50
Plum or Fruit Cobbler   51
Kentish Cherry Pancakes   52
Apple Snow   53
Kentish Fruit and Cream Compote   54
Gooseberry or Fresh Fruit Fool   55
Cherries in Kirsch   56
Cherries in Red Wine   57
Kentish Honeyed Fruit Salad   58

SCONES
Kent Apple and Cheese Scone Round   59
Dover Splits   60

CAKES and BISCUITS
Apple Gingerbread   61
Kentish Huffkins   62
Tunbridge Wells Cakes   63
Brandy Snaps   64
Laura's Almond Macaroon Biscuits   65
Gran's Boiled Cake   66
Kentish Cake   67
Kentish Flead Cakes   67
Mother's Rock Cakes   68
Oast Cakes   69

SAUCES
Red Wine Sauce   70
Apple Sauce   70
Caper Sauce   71

PICKLES and JAMS
Pickled Kentish Cherries   72
Damson Cheese   73
Sarah's Marmalade   74
Kentish Cherry and Raspberry Jam   75
Green Tomato and Apple Chutney   76

DRINKS
Hop Beer   77
Parsnip Wine   78
Mulled Ale   79
To Brew Margate Ale   80

'Kent, Sir? Everybody knows Kent —
apples, cherries, hops and women.'

Mr. Jingle in *Pickwick Papers*
Charles Dickens

KENT

For centuries Kent has been known as the Garden of England. Medieval fruit farmers discovered that by describing their fields as gardens, the payment of tythes and taxes could be avoided. In springtime the countryside is a sea of pink and white blossom — promising a plentiful harvest of apples, cherries, plums and pears in the months to come. The mild climate and fertile soil provide ideal conditions for growing fruit, which is used locally in sweet puddings, pies and preserves, and also in pickles, chutneys or sauces to serve with chicken, pork and fish. Soft fruit, such as strawberries and raspberries — particularly in the Malling area with names such as Malling Exploit, Malling Promise and Malling Jewel — also thrive, and cob nuts are grown extensively. Today many Kentish farms sell fresh fruit and vegetables on a 'pick your own' basis, or from roadside stalls.

Another typically Kentish sight are the conical oast houses, which are used for drying hops. Hops were originally grown in Kent 2,000 years ago by the Romans, not for beer making but as a vegetable. The young shoots picked in May or June are very good served hot with melted butter, like asparagus. The hops were introduced again in the 16th century from the Continent for beer making. The river Medway became important in providing water for brewing and transporting the beer. Maidstone, the county town of Kent, was soon the centre of the industry. Originally the hops were dried on circular floors above a coal furnace; the distinctive cowl at the top of the oast house turned with the wind in order to provide good ventilation. Today the drying process is assisted by fans. When it is completed, the hops are sent to the breweries packed into large canvas bags called 'pockets'.

In Victorian times, with the advent of the railways reaching down into Kent, parties of women and children from the East End of London arrived each year in early September to pick the hops by hand. This continued until after the end of the Second World War. The hop pickers lived for several weeks in the hop gardens in shacks provided by the farmers, cooking such things as oast cakes over an open fire.

Kent has a long coast line, and most of the ports have small fishing fleets. Fish has always been a local speciality, and freshly caught fish can often be bought on the beach straight from the fishing boats. The most famous Kentish fish is the Dover sole. It is usually about 12 inches long and a large fish can weigh up to 6 lbs. Local people prefer it straight from the sea, simply grilled.

Kentish lamb is particularly succulent, and sheep grazing in the orchards is a traditional part of the landscape. Romney Marsh and Isle of Sheppy sheep are two famous breeds.

In Biddenden in Kent every Easter Monday small biscuits, stamped with the figures of two girls, are still distributed in the village. This is to commemorate the generosity of two sisters, Eliza and Mary Chulkhurst, Siamese twins, who were born in the year 1100. They died at the age of 34, and left a large plot of land to be used to help the poor.

Visitors to Kent will not be surprised, considering that the hop is one of the county's foremost crops, that Kent abounds in very attractive pubs, many with dried hops displayed above the bar. Their names often reflect the local produce — 'The Cob Tree', 'The Ewe and Lamb', 'The Cherry Tree', 'The Golding Hop', 'The Hop Pocket' and the 'Fisherman's Rest'.

'The Man of Kent' and 'The Kentish Man' reflect an interesting historical quirk. The river Medway is the traditional dividing line between the Men of Kent who live on the eastern bank, and the Kentish Men on the west.

CREAMED GREEN PEA SOUP

Serves 6

2 lbs (1 kg) green peas
1½ pints (900 ml/ 3¾ cups) stock (preferably bacon)
¾ pint (450 ml/ 2 cups) milk
1 onion
1 oz (25 g) butter
1 oz (25 g) cornflour
1 teaspoon chopped mint
Salt and pepper
¼ pint (150 ml/ ⅔ cup) double cream (optional)

Shell the peas.

Chop the onion.

Wash the pods.

Put them in a saucepan with the stock and onion and bring to the boil and then simmer for 30 minutes. Strain.

Return the stock to the saucepan.

Add the shelled peas and the mint.

Simmer gently until the peas are tender.

Rub through a sieve or blend in a liquidizer.

Mix the cornflour with the milk.

Put the pea purée, milk and butter back into the saucepan.

Season to taste with the salt and pepper.

Bring to the boil, stirring, and cook for a few minutes.

The consistency can be adjusted by adding milk or water as required.

Swirl the cream on the top of the soup just before serving.

ST. MARGARET'S BAY PRAWNS IN TOMATOES
Serves 4

The most famous starter using prawns is the well known Prawn Cocktail, but here is a more unusual 'beginning' to a meal.

Prawns can be found at low tide in the rock pools at St. Margaret's Bay, near Dover, and at other places around the Kent coast.

2 eggs
4 firm tomatoes
1 oz (25 g) butter
Salt and pepper
24 prawns, peeled
8 drops anchovy essence or to taste

Hard boil the eggs, shell and mash.

Cut the tomatoes in half and remove the flesh.

Melt the butter in a saucepan.

Add the tomato flesh and salt and pepper to taste.

Cook very gently for a few minutes until soft.

Purée the tomato mixture through a sieve or in a liquidizer.

Add the mashed hard boiled egg.

Stir in the anchovy essence.

Add the peeled prawns.

Pile the mixture into the tomato cases.

Serve on a bed of lettuce or watercress.

CREAMY SHRIMP TOASTS

Both brown and red shrimps are found in abundance round the Kent coast. The brown ones are considered to have the best flavour.

Serves 4 as a light snack. Serves 8 if toasts are cut in half and eaten as a starter before a main meal.

2 oz (50 g) butter
½ teaspoon anchovy essence
Salt and pepper
¾ pint (450 ml/ 2 cups) shrimps
½ pint (300 ml/ 1¼ cups) milk
1 oz (25 g) flour
2 tablespoons single cream
4 rounds of bread

Shell the shrimps.

Melt 1 oz butter in a small saucepan.

Stir in the flour to make roux and still stirring, cook for a few moments over a gentle heat.

Slowly add the milk to the roux.

Add the salt and pepper to taste.

Bring to the boil, and cook for 5 minutes, still stirring.

Add the shrimps (reserving a few for garnishing).

Add some of the anchovy essence. Stir in the cream.

Keep hot while preparing the toast.

Cream butter with drops of the anchovy essence.

Toast the bread and spread with the anchovy butter.

Spread the shrimp cream onto the toast.

Garnish with the remaining shrimps.

Serve very hot.

TWICE LAID

These Kentish fishcakes get their name from the fact that they can be made from left-over cod.

12 oz (350 g) cooked cod, flaked
1 lb (450 g) potatoes, mashed
A little milk
1 egg
Salt and pepper
Breadcrumbs
Fat for frying

Mix the fish with the potatoes.

Season to taste with salt and pepper.

Bind together with a little milk.

Shape the mixture into small cakes.

Dip into the beaten egg.

Coat with breadcrumbs.

Deep fry in hot fat until the fishcakes are golden brown.

Drain and serve.

WHITSTABLE OYSTERS

Whitstable is a small port famous since Roman times for oysters. Today oyster dredgers are kept busy, farming the 'Royal Whitstable Natwes', as the oysters are locally known.

Ask the fishmonger to open the oysters.

Serve in their shells, sprinkled with paprika or cayenne pepper.

Serve with wedges of lemon and thin brown bread and buter.

BAKED ROCHESTER SMELTS   Serves 4

These small fish are known as 'Cucumber fish' because of their unique smell. Handle gently as they break up easily. Smelts used to be a great delicacy, but they are now rather difficult to obtain. Smelts are salt water fish. They swim up river to spawn. They may be ordered from a fishmonger. Or substitute small trout.

8 smelts
Salt and pepper
Lemon juice
1 small shallot
1 oz (25 g) parsley
¼ teaspoon anchovy essence
2 oz (50 g) breadcrumbs
1 oz (25 g) butter or margarine
Lemon and parsley to decorate

Clean, wash and dry the fish.

Trim off the fins.

Lay the fish side by side in a buttered ovenproof dish.

Sprinkle with salt, pepper and lemon juice.

Cut up the shallot finely.

Mix the shallot with the anchovy essence, 1 teaspoon chopped parsley, and the breadcrumbs.

Spread the mixture over the fish.

Dot with the butter, cut into small pieces.

Cover the dish with greaseproof paper.

Bake in a moderate oven for 20 mintues.

Serve decorated with lemon wedges and parsley.

Oven: 350°F/180°C Gas Mark 4

MUSSELS IN WHITE WINE

Serves 4

This dish has been popular since the Middle Ages. Mussels abound around the Kent coast.

6 pts (3.5 litres/15 cups) mussels
½ pt (300 ml/ 1¼ cups) dry white wine
½ lb (225 g) onions
3 oz (75 g) butter
1½ oz (40 g) flour
¾ pt (450 ml/ 2 cups) milk
1 oz (25 g) parsley, chopped
7½ fl oz (225 ml/ 1 cup) double cream
Salt and pepper

Scrub and wash the mussels well, discarding any that are open or will not close when sharply tapped.

Put the wine in a saucepan and bring to the boil.

Add the mussels and simmer gently for 5 minutes until the mussels have all opened.

Lift out the mussels and remove the beards with a knife.

Take the mussels out of their shells.

Strain the wine stock through a fine sieve and retain.

Peel and chop the onions.

Cook gently in half the butter until soft.

Melt the remaining butter and stir in the flour.

Continue stirring without browning, for a few minutes, gradually adding in the mussel stock.

Warm the milk, add it to the stock with the onions, and simmer for a few minutes.

Add the mussels, chopped parsley and cream, and season to taste with salt and pepper.

Heat over a gentle heat without boiling.

Serve in individual bowls.

DOVER SOLE IN WHITE WINE   Serves 4

8 fillets of Dover sole
Lemon juice
½ pint (300 ml/ 1 ¼ cups) white wine
½ pint (300 ml/ 1 ¼ cups) fish stock
1½ oz (40 g) butter or margarine
1 oz (25 g) flour, plain or self-raising
Salt and pepper
2 oz (50 g) peeled shrimps
Parsley to decorate

Sprinkle the fillets with salt, pepper and lemon juice.

Starting at the thick end roll the fillets up neatly.

Place the fillets in a greased fireproof dish.

Mix the white wine with the stock.

Pour the liquid over the fillets.

Cover the dish with greaseproof paper.

Bake in a moderate oven for about 15 minutes.

Just before the fish is cooked, melt the butter in a saucepan.

Stir in the flour to make a roux.

Cook for a moment or two, stirring all the time.

Remove the fish from the oven, and strain off the liquid.

Add the liquid gradually to the roux, stirring continuously.

Bring to the boil and then simmer for several minutes, until the sauce thickens, still stirring.

Add the shrimps.

Adjust seasoning to taste.

Pour the sauce over the fillets.

Garnish with parsley before serving.

SEAFLOWER

A seafood dish of fresh sea bass filled with white crab meat flavoured with saffron and fresh chives and covered by a light white wine sauce, invented by Clive Kingston of The Royal Hotel, Deal, in memory of the *Seaflower* which was sunk of the Goodwin sands in the English Channel in 1873.

The Royal Hotel in Deal which is right on the promenade, overlooking the Goodwin sands, has been an important hostelry for nearly 300 years. It was named The Royal after a visit by Queen Adelaide in the 19th century. Lord Nelson and Lady Hamilton frequently met there for a romantic tryst. Turner painted the hotel in a famous water colour dated 1825.

1½-2 lbs (675g - 1 kg) sea bass
White crab meat
Chives
½ oz (15 g) saffron
2 tablespoons clarified butter (see method)
Salt and black pepper
White sauce
4 fl oz (6 tablespoons / ½ cup) white wine

Prepare the bass, leaving the head on.

Mix the white crab meat with fresh chopped chives and saffron.

Stuff the bass with the mixture.

Put into cooking foil with two tablespoons of clarified butter.

Season with salt and black pepper, and seal.

Cook in a medium oven for approximately 25 minutes.

Prepare a white sauce and add the white wine.

Season to taste.

Reduce to double cream consistency.

Serve with the sauce poured over the fish.

Oven: 350°F/180°C Gas Mark 4

To clarify butter:

Heat slightly salted butter gently in a saucepan, stirring all the time until the liquid foams.

Cook without browning, until the foaming stops.

Allow to stand for a few minutes, but not to solidify.

Strain through muslin, before using.

BEER BATTER

Can be used to coat fish, chicken or vegetables, before frying in hot fat until browned.

4 oz (100 g) flour
½ pt (300 ml/ 1¼ cups) beer
½ teaspoon salt
2 oz (50 g) butter
2 eggs

Sift the flour and salt together into a bowl.

Separate the eggs and beat the yolks.

Stir in the beer.

Add the liquid to the flour.

Stir gently until blended.

Melt the butter and add it to the mixture.

Allow to stand for at least 30 minutes.

Beat the egg whites until stiff but not dry and fold them into the mixture.

PHEASANT IN PORT WINE

Serves 3-4

1 pheasant
8 oz (255 g) carrots
1 shallot
8 oz (225 g) pork sausage meat
4 oz (100 g) calf's liver
1 oz (25 g) butter or margarine
Salt and pepper
¼ pt (150 ml/ ⅔ cup) port wine
6 rashers of streaky bacon
1 oz (25 g) flour
Gravy browning

Slice the liver thinly.

Put the pheasant and the liver in a deep bowl and pour over the wine. Leave to marinate for at least 8 hours.

Take out the liver from the marinade. Fry it gently in the butter until tender. Retain the butter.

Put the liver through a mincer twice.

Mix the minced liver and the butter it was cooked in with the sausage meat.

Remove the bird from the marinade, and retain the liquid.

Stuff the bird with the mixture.

Peel and slice the carrots thinly.

Put the sliced carrots in the bottom of a casserole.

Lay the pheasant on top of the carrots, and cover the breast with the bacon.

Season the marinade with salt and pepper to taste, and pour over the pheasant.

Cover the casserole with the lid or tin foil.

Cook in a moderate oven for 45 minutes, remove the lid and cook for a further 15 minutes.

Put the pheasant, bacon and carrots on a serving dish.

Use the gravy in the casserole, thickened with a little flour or cornflour, to make a thick brown sauce, with browning.

Oven: 375°F/190°C Gas Mark 5

KENTISH CHICKEN PUDDING   Serves 4

In the middle ages, chickens were kept only for egg-laying. By the time they were killed, they were so old and tough, only long boiling would make them edible. This recipe is a modern version of the old dish using today's tender young birds.

4 chicken portions
8 oz (225 g) salt belly of pork, diced
1 lb (450 g) suet pastry
¼ pint (150 ml/ ⅔ cup) chicken stock
1 onion, chopped
1 teaspoon parsley, finely chopped
Salt and pepper to taste

Remove the skin and bones from the chicken.

Cut the meat into pieces.

Mix together the chicken, pork, onion, salt, pepper and parsley.

Line a 2 pt greased pudding basin with ¾ of the suet pastry.

Add the meat mixture and pour in the chicken stock.

Cover with the remaining pastry rolled out as a lid.

Cover the basin with greaseproof paper or foil.

Steam for 2 hours.

Turn out the pudding.

Serve with parsley sauce.

CHICKEN IN HOCHEE

This recipe is a favourite of The Shant Hotel at East Sutton, near Maidstone, in the heart of the beautiful Kent countryside. The Hotel has a reputation for good food, and specialises in using fresh home grown vegetables and local produce.

3 lb (1.5 kg) chicken
4 oz (100 g) white grapes
2 tablespoons chopped sage and parsley (mixed)
1 clove of garlic
¾ pint (450 ml) chicken stock
½ teaspoon caster sugar
½ teaspoon cinnamon
Salt and pepper to taste

Remove pips from the grapes.

Coat in herbs and crushed garlic.

Stuff the bird with the grapes, and put in an ovenproof dish.

Pour on the stock.

Braise in a moderate oven for approximately 1 hour 45 minutes.

When cooked, sprinkle with sugar and cinnamon.

Return to the oven to allow the sugar and cinnamon to form a glaze.

Put the chicken on a serving dish.

Reduce the stock to make a sauce.

Serve sprinkled with parsley and garnished with grapes.

Oven: 350°F/180°C Gas Mark 4

CASSEROLE OF RABBIT WITH RED WINE

Serves 4

4 joints of rabbit
2 oz (50 g) flour
8 oz (225 g) streaky bacon
¾ pt (450 ml/ 2 cups) stock
2 medium onions
2 shallots
2 carrots
A pinch of mace
5 cloves
Salt and black pepper to taste
Teaspoon of allspice
½ teaspoon of finely grated lemon peel
½ pt (300 ml/ 1¼ cups) red wine or claret
1 bay leaf
A little oil for frying
Cornflour for thickening

Coat the rabbit joints with the flour.

Cut the bacon into pieces and fry in a frying pan in hot oil.

Remove the bacon when cooked.

Fry the rabbit joints until golden brown.

Put the rabbit and the bacon into a saucepan with the stock.

Slice the onions, shallots and carrots. Fry them in the bacon fat until soft.

Add the onions, shallots, carrots, mace, cloves, seasoning, allspice, lemon peel and bay leaf to the rabbit.

Bring to the boil and gently simmer for about 1½ hours or until the rabbit is tender. If the gravy is too thin, thicken with cornflour.

About 20 minutes before serving, add the red wine or claret.

STEAK AND OYSTER PUDDING   Serves 6

A version of the famous British steak and kidney pudding, this steak and oyster pudding was traditionally made in Kent during the Whitstable oyster season.

Suet puddings, both sweet and savoury, like pork and apple pudding, or steak and kidney pudding, were often tied in cloth and boiled in the copper — also used for boiling the clothes. Housewives had a special long handled fork to enable them to get the pudding safely out of the boiling water.

1½ lb (675 g) suet pastry
1½ lb (675 g) stewing steak
½ lb (225 g) ox kidney
4 oz (100 g) mushrooms
6 oysters (or more if liked)
3 onions
2 oz (50 g) flour
Salt and pepper
¼ pt (150 ml/ ⅔ cup) meat stock
¼ pt (150 ml/ ⅔ cup) sherry

Cut up the stewing steak and kidney into neat pieces.

Peel and slice the mushrooms and onions.

Cut the oysters into small pieces.

Put the 2 oz (50 g) flour into a small basin and season with salt and pepper.

Roll the steak and kidney pieces in the seasoned flour until well coated.

Grease a 2 lb (1 kg) pudding basin.

Line the basin with ¾ of the suet pastry allowing the pastry to hang over the rim. Set the rest aside for a lid.

Mix the steak and kidney, mushrooms, onions and oysters together.

Pack the ingredients into the pudding.

Mix the meat stock and sherry together.

Pour the stock onto the pudding.

Turn the edges of the pastry over the meat, all round, and damp the edges. Cover with the remaining pastry. (If the lid is put on by this method there is no risk of any gravy escaping).

Tie down the pudding securely either with a greased tin foil, or greaseproof paper and a floured pudding cloth.

Steam for 3-4 hours.

SHANT STEWED STEAK   Serves 8

2 ½ lbs (1.25 kg) chuck steak
2 level tablespoons flour
1 onion, sliced
¼ pint (150 ml/ ⅔ cup) port
¼ pint (150 ml/ ⅔ cup) stout
2 tablespoons vinegar
8 oz (225 g) baby carrots
8 oz (225 g) chopped leek
8 oz (225 g) button mushrooms
Salt and pepper to taste

Cut the steak into large pieces.

Rub the meat on both sides with the flour and seasoning.

Place in a casserole.

Lay the onion over the top.

Pour over the liquids.

Cover with foil and stew for 3 hours in a moderate oven.

After 2 hours add the carrots, leeks and mushrooms.

Serve with creamed potatoes.

Oven: 325°F/160°C Gas Mark 3

HODGE PODGE

8 oz (225 g) dried green peas
1 lb (450 g) best end neck of mutton
1 lb (450 g) shin of beef
2 onions
4 carrots
4 sticks of celery
1 small turnip (if liked)
1½ pints (900 ml/ 3¾ cups) beef stock
Salt and pepper

Soak the dried peas overnight in water to cover.

Cut the mutton into neat cutlets removing superfluous fat.

Cut the shin of beef into small chunks.

Slice the onions.

Cut the turnip, celery and carrots into large pieces.

Put the meat, dried peas, onions, celery and carrots into a saucepan.

Cover with the stock and season to taste with salt and pepper.

Bring to the boil, and simmer gently for about 2 hours until the meat and vegetables are tender.

Remove the carrot, celery and turnip pieces and mash them together.

Return to the hodge podge.

Serve in a hot dish.

BOILED LEG OF LAMB IN CAPER SAUCE

Isle of Sheppey sheep are famed, and Romney Marsh is internationally known for is hardy breed which produces highly regarded meat from extremely poor pasture. Popular and useful all over the world for this ability, these sheep are exported in considerable numbers, mainly through Sheep Fairs held regularly at such towns as Rye, Biddenden, Ashford and the county town of Maidstone.

Romney Marsh, which has been reclaimed from over the sea over the centuries, was also notorious for smuggling in the early 19th century. Only those born and bred in the district knew the way through the maze of inland channels.

1 leg of lamb
1 bouquet garni of mixed herbs
Salt and pepper
2 onions
4 carrots
1 or 2 turnips (if liked)

Weigh the joint and calculate the cooking time.

The cooking time is the same as for roast lamb. Allow 20-25 minutes per lb plus an extra 20-25 minutes.

Bring sufficient water to cover the joint to the boil in a saucepan.

Add the bouquet garni and seasoning to taste.

Bring back to the boil and skim off any fat.

Reduce heat and simmer for the required cooking time.

Peel the vegetables and slice.

About 30 minutes before the end of cooking time, add the vegetables.

Remove the bouquet garni before serving.

Place the meat on a serving dish, and surround with the vegetables.

Serve with creamed potatoes and caper sauce (see recipe).

HERB PIE

A delightful change from the more usual steak and kidney pie, the cheap bacon pieces make the expensive chunk steak go further. It was therefore also called Poor Man's Veal and Ham Pie.

1 lb (450 g) chuck steak
8 oz (225 g) bacon pieces
1 teaspoon mixed dried herbs
Salt and pepper
½ pt (300 ml/ 1¼ cups) beef stock (or enough to just cover the meat)
2 teaspoons cornflour
6 oz shortcrust pastry
A little oil

Cut up the steak and the bacon pieces into neat chunks.

Brown the meat for a few minutes in the hot oil in a saucean.

Add the dried herbs and the stock to just cover the meat.

Season with salt and pepper.

Bring to the boil and simmer gently for about 1½ hours until tender.

Thicken the gravy with the cornflour, while still hot.

Put the meat and gravy into a pie dish.

Cover with shortcrust pastry, making a hole in the centre for the steam to escape.

Bake in a hot oven for about 20 minutes until the pastry is golden brown.

Delicious served with mustard.

Oven: 400°F/200°C Gas Mark 6

BEEF IN BEER

1 lb (450 g) stewing steak
2 oz (50 g) seasoned flour
Oil
2 carrots
2 oz (50 g) mushrooms
2 onions
2 or 3 sticks of celery
1 tablespoon tomato sauce
½ pint (300 ml/ 1¼ cups) beef stock
½ pint (300 ml/ 1¼ cups) beer
Salt and pepper
Bay leaf

Cut the meat into neat 1 inch chunks.

Roll the meat in the seasoned flour.

Chop up the carrots, celery, mushrooms and onions.

Fry the onions in the hot oil until soft.

Add the other vegetables and fry until golden brown.

Put in a casserole or saucepan.

Fry the meat in the hot fat until golden brown.

Add the meat to the vegetables.

Mix the beef stock with the beer and pour over the meat and vegetables.

Add the bay leaf.

Bring to the boil and then simmer on top of the stove in a covered saucepan for 2 hours or until the meat is tender.

Or bake in a moderate oven for the same time.

If stock requires further thickening add 1 oz of cornflour mixed with 1 tablespoon of the stock, and cook for a few minutes longer.

Remove the bay leaf before serving.

PORK CHOPS IN BEER

Serves 6

6 pork chops
¾ pint (450 ml/ 2 cups) light ale
4 medium onions
2 oz (50 g) butter or margarine
½ pint (300 ml/ 1 ¼ cups) stock
2 oz (50 g) cornflour
Salt and pepper
Bouquet garni

Put the chops in a casserole.

Pour on the ale and leave to marinate for 1 hour.

Peel and slice the onions.

Melt the butter in a frying pan.

Fry the onions gently until soft.

Put the onions on top of the pork chops and ale.

Add the stock, thickened with the cornflour.

Add the bouquet garni and season to taste.

Cover and cook in a moderate oven for 1½ hours or until the chops are tender.

Oven: 350°F/180°C Gas Mark 4

PORK AND APPLE PIE

Serves 4

1 lb (450 g) pork
12 oz (350 g) cooking apples
1 oz (25 g) caster sugar
Sage
Salt and black pepper
¼ pt (150 ml/ ⅔ cup) meat stock
6 oz (175 g) shortcrust pastry
Beaten egg to glaze

Cut the pork into pieces.

Peel, core and slice the apples.

Put a generous layer of meat at the bottom of a pie dish.

Season with salt and pepper.

Sprinkle with a little chopped fresh or dried sage.

Next put a thin layer of sliced apples.

Lightly sprinkle the apple with sugar.

Continue with the layers as before until all the ingredients are used, and the dish is full.

Pour on the stock — the juice from the apples will be added to this as the dish cooks.

Roll out the pastry on a floured board to make a lid.

Cover the dish with the pastry.

Make a slit in the centre.

Brush the pastry with a beaten egg.

Bake in a moderate hot oven for 1½ hours.

Protect the pastry with greaseproof paper after about 30 minutes or when golden brown.

Oven: 375°F/190°C Gas Mark 5

TONBRIDGE BRAWN

Serves 6

1 pig's head
Salt
Cayenne pepper
¼ pt (150 ml/ ⅔ cup) white wine
2 bay leaves
Water

Ask the butcher to chop up the pigs head.

Put the meat in a saucepan with the wine and add sufficient water to cover.

Add the bay leaves.

Bring to the boil. Skim if necessary.

Put the lid on the saucepan, and simmer gently until meat comes away easily from the bones.

Allow to cool, then strain off the liquid, and save.

Remove the meat from the bones and cut into neat pieces.

Discard bones, fat, skin, gristle and bay leaves.

Put the meat back into the liquid and leave until cold.

Remove any fat that has collected on the surface.

Put the now jellied meat back into the saucepan.

Melt over a gentle heat and season with salt and pepper.

Simmer for 10 minutes.

Pour the mixture into a mould, wetted with cold water.

There should be only sufficient liquid to cover the meat.

Take off any excess.

Leave in a cold place or refrigerator for a few hours to set.

Turn the brawn out on to a serving dish.

Decorate with parsley.

FAGGOTS

Faggots were known as 'Poor Man's Goose' and are believed to date back to Roman times. They used to be sold hot on Saturday nights in West Street and Pudding lane, Maidstone. In the 19th century, they were sold at most butchers shops. Recipes for faggots vary around the country, but basically they were an ideal way of using up the left overs after a pig was killed.

Traditionally they were served with pease pudding. But they are delicious cut into slices and served hot or cold, and also excellent fried with eggs for breakfast.

8 oz (225 g) raw liver
2 medium sized onions
2 rashers bacon
3 slices brown bread
2 eggs
2 oz (50 g) flour
½ pint (300 ml/ 1¼ cups) milk
Salt and pepper
½ teaspoon sage

Beat the eggs together.

Make a batter beating the eggs and ¼ pint of milk into the flour.

Add the salt and pepper to taste, and the sage.

Mince the liver, onions and bacon together.

Soak the bread in the remainder of the milk.

Mix with the minced ingredients.

Stir into the batter thoroughly.

Put into a greased tin.

Cover with tin foil lid.

Stand tin in a larger tin of water.

Cook in a hot oven for about 1 hour.

Oven: 400°F/200°C Gas Mark 6

CREAMED CABBAGE

1 cabbage
1 oz (25 g) margarine
½ oz (15 g) flour
Water
Salt and pepper
A little cream or milk
Nutmeg to taste

Wash and prepare the cabbage.

Cut the leaves up roughly.

Bring to the boil enough salted water to barely cover the cabbage.

Drop the cabbage into the water.

Put on the saucepan lid, and boil rapidly for 10 minutes.

Drain well, retaining the cabbage water.

Melt the magarine in a small saucepan.

Stir in the flour.

Bring the cabbage water to the boil, and stir it into the roux to make a smooth thick sauce.

Simmer for a few minutes.

Add a little cream or milk.

Season with pepper and a dash of nutmeg.

Stir the cabbage gently into the sauce until well coated.

Serve very hot.

BRUSSELS SPROUTS WITH CHESTNUTS

Serves 4

1½ lb (675 g) Brussels sprouts
½ lb (225 g) chestnuts
1 pint (600 ml/ 2½ cups) water
½ pt (300 ml/ 1¼ cups) stock (chicken)
1 onion
1 clove
Bouquet garni
Salt and pepper
1 oz (25 g) butter
1 tablespoon lemon juice

Peel off the outer skin of the chestnuts.

Put them into ¼ pint (150 ml/ ⅔ cup) boiling water for a few minutes.

Remove, and take off the inner skin.

Put the chestnuts in a saucepan with the stock, the peeled onion stuck with the clove, and the bouquet garni.

Bring to the boil and simmer for 1 hour, or until the chestnuts are tender. Strain.

Cook the prepared sprouts in about ¾ pint (450 ml/ 2 cups) boiling salted water for about 8 minutes. Drain well.

While still hot, mix carefully with the chestnuts avoiding breaking the sprouts.

Melt the butter in a saucepan.

Toss the sprouts and chestnuts in the melted butter, and the lemon juice.

Serve immediately.

KENTISH CAULIFLOWER WITH SHRIMP SAUCE

Serves 4

Cauliflowers are grown in large fields on the approach to Margate, Ramsgate and Broadstairs.

High on a cliff overlooking the attractive Victorian seaside town of Broadstairs on the Isle of Thanet in Kent, is Bleak House. Here Charles Dickens lived when he was writing his novel David Copperfield. A Dickens Festival is held in the town during mid June.

Shrimp sauce is also excellent served with fish. It is traditional with turbot.

1 large cauliflower
2 oz (50 g) butter
2 oz (50 g) flour
¾ pt (450 ml/ 2 cups) milk
1 tablespoon lemon juice
2½ fl oz (4 tbsp/ ⅓ cup) double cream
Salt and pepper to taste
8 oz (225 g) peeled shrimps

Wash and prepare the cauliflower. Leave whole.

Cook for 15 minutes in boiling salted water, to which a little lemon has been added (to keep the cauliflower white).

Strain the cauliflower and keep warm in a serving dish.

Melt the butter in a saucepan.

Stir in the flour and cook without browning for 3 minutes.

Add the milk, stirring, and bring to the boil.

Simmer gently over a low heat, still stirring, until the sauce thickens.

Season to taste.

Stir in the lemon juice, cream and shrimps.

Heat for a few minutes longer without boiling.

Pour the sauce over the cauliflower and serve immediately.

CAULIFLOWER CHEESE FROM THE ISLE OF THANET

Serves 4

The Isle of Thanet is only an island in name today, but in Roman times, was separated from the mainland by the Rivers Stour and Wantsum. Cauliflowers are grown in large fields on the approach to Margate, Ramsgate and Broadstairs.

1 large cauliflower
2 oz (50 g) butter or margarine
2 oz (50 g) flour
1 pt (600 ml/ 2½ cups) milk
5 oz (150 g) cheese
Salt and pepper
Breadcrumbs

Put the prepared cauliflower florets into boiling salted water, and simmer rapidly for about 10 minutes until soft. Strain when ready.

While the cauliflower is cooling, grate the cheese.

Melt the butter or margarine in another saucepan.

Stir in the flour to make a roux.

Cook stirring all the time, for a few moments.

Continuing to stir gradually add the milk.

Bring to the boil, and simmer until the sauce thickens.

Season with salt and pepper to taste.

Add the grated cheese, retaining 1 oz (25 g).

Mix the cooked cauliflower into the cheese sauce, stirring gently.

Put the mixture into a fireproof dish.

Sprinkle the top evenly with the grated cheese and breadcrumbs.

Brown the dish under a hot grill or in a hot oven for about 10 minutes until golden brown.

KENTISH RAREBIT

Makes 6 rounds

There are several versions of rarebit. This was a popular snack with the friut pickers in the orchards of Kent at the turn of the century.

2 oz (50 g) butter or margarine
3 dessert apples
12 oz (350 g) Cheddar cheese
Pepper to taste
Rounds of toasted bread

Peel, core and slice the apples.

Grate the cheese.

Melt the butter or margarine in a saucepan.

Gently cook the apples in the melted butter, but do not let them brown.

Add the grated cheese and pepper and mix well together.

Spread onto the rounds of toast and brown under a hot grill until the mixture is bubbling.

KENTISH CHEESE PASTIES

8 oz (225 g) shortcrust pastry
4 oz (100 g) cheese, grated
1 egg (beaten)
Salt and cayenne pepper to taste

Roll out the pastry, thinly.

Using an upturned saucer as a guide, cut out rounds.

Pile the grated cheese equally in the centre of the pastry rounds.

Sprinkle with salt and pepper.

Dampen the pastry edges.

Fold up and press edges together.

Brush the pasties with beaten egg.

Bake for 15-20 minutes until golden brown.

Oven: 425°F/220°C Gas Mark 7

CHEESE AND APPLE PIE

Serves 4

6 oz (175 g) shortcrust pastry
1½ lb (675 g) cooking apples
6 oz (175 g) cheddar cheese
2 oz (50 g) sugar, or to taste
A little water

Peel, core and slice the apples.

Cut the cheese into thin slices.

Cover the bottom of a 1½ pt (900 ml/3¾ cups) pie dish with a layer of the sliced apples.

Sprinkle evenly with the sugar and cover with the sliced cheese.

Finish with another layer of apple.

Roll out the short crust pastry to make a lid for the pie dish.

Damp the edges of the dish with water.

Cover with the pastry lid.

Mark the edge with the back of a fork to make a pattern.

Bake in a hot oven for 10-15 minutes, then lower the temperture to moderate. Bake for a further 30 minutes until the apples are cooked.

Oven: 450°F/230°C Gas Mark 8 for 10-15 minutes
Reduce to: 350°F/180°C Gas Mark 4 for 30 minutes

GRAN GOMAR'S CHEESE SUPER DISH

Serves 3-4

This excellent cheese dish rises like a soufflé.

4 oz (100 g) white bread
6 oz (175 g) Cheddar cheese
¾ pint (450 ml/ 2 cups) milk
1 oz (25 g) butter or margarine
2 eggs
Salt and pepper
A little mustard

Crumb the bread against a grater using one day old bread.

Grate the cheese.

Mix the breadcrumbs and grated cheese together.

Put the milk and butter in a saucepan.

Warm the milk and butter into a saucepan.

Pour mixture over dry ingredients.

Beat the eggs together.

Add salt, pepper and a little dry mustard to taste.

Mix altogether.

Put the mixture into a soufflé dish.

Bake in the oven for about 20 minutes until golden brown and well risen.

Serve with mixed salad.

Oven: 400°F/200°C Gas Mark 6

COB NUT AND CHEESE SAVOURY BAKE

Serves 4

There are cob nut orchards in Kent.

4 oz (100 g) cob nuts, shelled
4 oz (100 g) lentils
1 oz (25 g) butter or margarine
2 oz (50 g) breadcrumbs
2 oz (50 g) grated cheese
Salt and pepper

Wash the lentils, removing any black ones.

Soak the lentils in cold water overnight or for a minimum of an hour.

Bring to the boil and simmer until tender.

Strain off the liquid.

Rub the lentils through a sieve, or blend in a liquidizer.

Grate or chop the nuts finely.

Mix the nuts and lentils together.

Season with salt and pepper.

Put the mixture into a greased pie dish.

Sprinkle the top with the breadcrumbs.

Dot with the butter cut into small pieces.

Sprinkle on the grated cheese.

Bake in a hot oven for 30 minutes.

Oven: 400°F/200°C Gas Mark 6

FLOATING ISLAND

This exotic floating trifle was popular at feasts and important dinner parties, particulary during the 17th century. It would certainly have been served at the great Kentish houses, like Leeds Castle, Knole, Penshurst and Hever, once the home of Anne Boleyn. Early recipes used a whipped syllabub in place of the fruit purée and cream to float the 'island', and the foam from the syllabub as a topping. The 'island' itself was made of bread instead of sponge.

The 'island' should float on top of the fruit purée, but even if it sinks, the pudding tastes delicious.

1 lb (450 g) raspberries or strawberries (fresh or frozen)
   Reserve a few whole fruits for decoration
8 inch sponge cake (light — made without fat)
2 tablespoons sherry
4 oz (100 g) jam, raspberry or strawberry
4 oz (100 g) blanched almonds, chopped
1 pint (600 ml/ 2½ cups) double cream
4 oz (100 g) caster sugar
½ teaspoon vanilla essence

Purée the raspberries or strawberries.

Beat half the cream.

Blend the fruit purée and juice with the cream.

Pour onto a flat serving dish.

Cut the sponge cake into three layers.

Spread each layer with jam and sprinkle with almonds.

Lay the first layer lightly on the centre of the purée.

Lightly put on the other layers to reassemble the cake.

Pour the sherry over the cake.

Whip the remaining cream with the sugar and vanilla essence and pile on top of the cake.

Decorate with a few whole raspberries or strawberries.

Best if chilled for an hour before serving.

NEW YEAR'S PUDDING

Serves 6

8 oz (225 g) bought trifle sponges or plain sandwich cake
8 oz (225 g) mincemeat
1 tablespoon brandy (if liked)
1 pint (600 ml/ 2½ cups) milk
4 eggs
2 oz (50 g) caster sugar
2 drops vanilla essence

Grease a 2 pint pudding basin.

Cut the trifle sponges or sandwich cake into fingers and line the bottom of the basin.

Continue until about half way up the sides of the basin.

Add the brandy to the mincemeat.

Put a layer of mincemeat in the bottom of the basin followed by a layer of sponge.

Continue in layers, finishing with a sponge layer to make a lid for the pudding.

Beat the eggs together.

Gently heat the milk avoiding boiling, and pour over the beaten eggs. Stir.

Add the sugar and vanilla essence. Stir.

Pour the milk mixture over the pudding.

Cover the top of the basin with a kitchen foil lid.

Stand the basin in a tin with high sides and pour in hot water to come ⅔ up the sides of the basin.

Bake on centre shelf of slow oven for 1½ hours or until the custard is set.

Remove from the oven and turn out on to a serving plate.

Serve hot with lightly whipped cream.

Oven: 300°F/150°C Gas Mark 2

KENT WELL PUDDING

This delicious pudding looks like a huge apple dumpling, but has a buttery lemon pond inside. It was traditionally eaten on Palm Sunday.

8 oz (225 g) self-raising flour
¼ teaspoon salt
4 oz (100 g) shredded suet
4 fl oz (6 tablespoons/ ½ cup) iced water
4 oz (100 g) butter, diced
4 oz (100 g) demerara sugar
1 large lemon
2 oz (50 g) currants or sultanas

Sift the flour and salt into a bowl.

Add the shredded suet and mix lightly with a fork.

Make a well in the centre and add the water, a little at a time, to make a soft dough.

Knead the dough lightly on a floured surface until it is free of cracks and roll it out to a thickness of about ¼ inch.

Cut a quarter segment and set it aside for the lid.

Use the remaining dough to line a well buttered pudding basin (1½ pts).

Put half the diced butter in the bottom of the basin.

Prick the lemon all over with the skewer and sit upright in the butter.

Cover it with the remaining butter and the sugar.

Sprinkle with the currants or sultanas.

Roll out reserved dough for the lid, dampen the edges and press it gently into place.

Cover the basin with a layer of greaseproof paper and foil. Tie down.

Stand the basin in a saucepan and pour in boiling water to come a third of the way up.

Cover the pan tightly and simmer for 3½ hours — topping up with water from time to time and never allowing it to go off the boil.

Rest the pudding for a moment or two before turning into a deep plate — make sure each serving includes a slice of the lemon.

ROCHESTER SYRUP PUDDING   Serves 4

This pudding is known by various names: Rochester, Patriotic, and Steamed Treacle. Black treacle may be used in place of golden syrup.

8 oz (225 g) self-raising flour
4 oz (100 g) butter or margarine
4 oz (100 g) sugar
2 beaten eggs
1 tablespoon milk
3 oz (75 g) golden syrup
A pinch of salt
A little milk

Cream the butter or margarine with the sugar.

Add the eggs.

Fold in the sieved flour and the pinch of salt.

Mix to a soft dropping consistency with the milk.

Put a layer of syrup in the bottom of a greased pudding basin.

Spoon over the mixture.

Cover the basin with greaseproof paper or foil.

Steam for 1½ hours.

Turn out.

Serve with extra warmed syrup or custard.

KENTISH PUDDING PIE

Serves 4

Also known as Lenten Pudding Pie. This recipe was so named because it is partly boiled, and partly baked in the oven. It was popular during Lent when no meat could be served. Instead of one big pie, Kentish Pudding Pies were sometimes made individually.

8 oz (225 g) shortcrust pastry
2 oz (50 g) ground rice
1 pt (600 ml/ 2½ cups) milk
2 oz (50 g) butter or margarine
1 oz (25 g) caster sugar
2 eggs
A pinch of spice
2 oz (50 g) currants
2 bay leaves
Nutmeg

Line a shallow greased pie dish with the pastry.

Mix the ground rice to a smooth cream with a little cold milk in a small basin or cup.

Put the two bay leaves and the rest of the milk into a saucepan and bring to the boil.

Put the lid on the saucepan and simmer for 10 minutes.

Remove the bay leaves, stir the ground rice mixture into the hot milk, and simmer for 3 minutes, stirring.

Stir in the sugar, spice and butter. Allow to cool slightly.

Beat the eggs together. Add the beaten eggs to the mixture, and pour into the pastry lined dish.

Sprinkle with currants, stirring them gently into the mixture, then scatter grated nutmeg over the top of the pudding.

Bake in a moderate oven for 30 minutes until golden brown and the rice custard is firm.

Serve either hot or cold.

Oven: 350°F/180°C Gas Mark 4

APPLE PIE

The plate pie, with pastry base and top and fruit filling, is the earliest type of fruit pie.

8 oz (225 g) apples
2 oz (50 g) sugar
8 oz (225 g) shortcrust pastry

Peel, core and slice the apples.

Divide the pastry into two.

Roll out to fit an 8 inch greased pie plate.

Line the plate with pastry.

Cover with the fruit.

Sprinkle with sugar.

Trim the pastry and seal the edges.

Make a slit in the top of the pie.

Bake for 15 minutes in a hot oven, then reduce for a further 30 minutes.

When cooked dredge with sugar and serve hot or cold.

Other fruit pies can be made by the same method.

Blackberry and Apple — Use 4 oz of each fruit.

Plum — Use ½ lb stoned plums.

Rhubard — Use ½ lb rhubarb, diced.

Cherry — Use ½ lb cherries, stoned.

Damson and Apple — Use 4 oz damsons, stoned, and 4 ozs sliced apples.

Oven: 425°F/220°C Gas Mark 7
Reduce to: 350°F/180°C Gas Mark 4

SPONGE HEDGEHOG

Hedgehog puddings were popular in Victorian times.

8 oz (225 g) self-raising flour, sieved
4 oz (100 g) margarine or butter
4 oz (100 g) caster sugar
2 eggs
2-3 tablespoons white wine
¾ pt (450 ml/ 2 cups) thick custard
2 oz (50 g) almonds

Cream the margarine and sugar together well.

Beat the eggs together.

Beat into the creamed mixture a little at a time.

Fold in the sieved flour.

Put the mixture into an oval greased tin.

Bake in a moderate oven for 30 minutes.

Remove from oven.

Turn out on to a plate when cool.

Spoon the wine slowly over the cake allowing it to soak in.

Cover the cake with the custard.

Blanch the almonds in hot water.

Peel and split.

Place the almonds lengthwise in rows over the pudding to create a 'porcupine' effect.

Oven: 350°F/180°C Gas Mark 4

RHUBARB HEDGEHOG

2 lb (1 kg) rhubarb
4 oz (100 g) caster sugar
1 lemon
2 oz (50 g) butter or margarine
¾ oz (20 g) gelatine
2 oz (50 g) almonds

Cut the prepared rhubarb into small chunks.

Stew very gently with the sugar, without water, until soft.

Rub through a sieve or liquidizer.

Grate the lemon rind, and squeeze.

Stir in the grated rind and lemon juice.

Warm the butter slightly.

Add it to the fruit mixture, and beat until well mixed.

Dissolve the gelatine in a little hot water and stir well into
the mixture.

Rinse out with cold water an oval shaped fluted decorative
mould.

Pour in the fruit mixture.

Put in the refrigerator or a cold place to set.

Blanch the almonds in hot water, then peel and split them.

Turn the pudding out of the mould on to a serving dish.

Stick the almonds lengthwise in rows along the top and down
the side to resemble the spines of a hedgehog.

LITTLE CANTERBURY PUDDINGS WITH GOOSEBERRIES
Makes 8-10 puddings

A number of cathedral towns had their own puddings. Generally speaking, they were all of a light sponge mixture type.

Canterbury was the Saxon town of Cantwarabyrig (the borough of the Men of Kent) when St. Augustine arrived on a mission from Rome in 597, and founded the first cathedral. Before that Canterbury was occupied by the Romans and in 300 BC was a settlement and centre of the Belgae tribe. Thomas à Becket was martyred in the cathedral in 1170.

8 oz (225 g) self-raising flour
5 oz (175 g) butter or margarine
5 oz (175 g) caster sugar
1 teaspoon mixed spice
2 eggs
A little milk to mix

Rub the fat into the flour until it resembles fine breadcrumbs.

Add the sugar.

Add the mixed spice.

Mix well together.

Beat the eggs into a little milk.

Mix into dry ingredients to make a dropping consistency.

Grease some small patty tins.

About three quarters fill the tins with the mixture.

Bake in a moderate oven for about 30 minutes until well risen and golden brown.

Turn out, allow to cool, and serve with a dish of stewed gooseberries and cream.

Also excellent with wine sauce (see recipe).

Oven: 350°F/180°C Gas Mark 4.

APPLE CHARLOTTE
Serves 4

This delicious pudding is sometimes called Brown Betty. It can be made half and half with blackberries and apples, if preferred.

2 lbs (1 kg) cooking apples
Cinnamon
4 oz (100 g) brown sugar
½ lemon
1 oz (25 g) butter
Slices of bread
2 oz (50 g) melted butter or margarine

Peel, core and slice the apples.

Squeeze the lemon.

Put the apples in a saucepan with the lemon juice, 3 oz (75 g) of the sugar and a little cinnamon to taste.

Cook the apples very gently over a low heat until they form a pulp.

Brush an ovenproof bowl with the melted butter.

Cut off the crusts from the bread.

Dip the bread in the melted butter. Retain enough bread to make a lid.

Use the bread to line the bottom and sides of the bowl.

Fill the bowl with the apple purée.

Put on the bread lid, which will have also been dipped in the melted butter. (Make sure that the pieces of bread overlap slightly in the bowl, or the apple purée will come through, and spoil the crisp outside).

Sprinkle the top of the pudding with the remaining sugar.

Bake in a moderate oven for 30 minutes.

Turn out to serve. Delicious with custard or cream.

Oven: 375°F/190°C Gas Mark 5

APPLE FRITTERS WITH BEER   Serves 4

4 oz (100 g) self-raising flour
A pinch of salt
1 tablespoon of oil
¼ pt (8 tablespoons/ ⅔ cups) beer (fresh or sour milk
   can be used for the batter, if preferred)
White of one egg
1 lb (450 g) cooking apples
Fat or oil for cooking
3 oz (75 g) caster sugar
½ teaspoon cinnamon

Peel and core the apples — using an apple corer, so that the
apples remain intact.

Cut the apples into rings, about ½ inch thick.

To make the batter:

(Once the batter is made, use immediately).

Sift the flour into a bowl.

Mix in the salt.

Add the oil.

Mix to a smooth cream with the beer liquid.

Whisk the egg white until stiff.

Stir into the batter.

Dip the apple rings into the batter, so that they are well
coated.

Deep fry in hot fat for about 5 minutes until golden brown.

Drain well.

Mix the cinnamon and caster sugar together.

Dust each fritter with the cinnamon sugar before serving.

PLUM OR FRUIT COBBLER

Serves 4

Cobblers were cooked on farmhouse ranges, when there was a surplus of fruit. Almost any fruit can be used, hard and soft — blackberries are especially good.

1 lb (450 g) plums
A little water
3 oz (75 g) brown sugar
8 oz (225 g) self raising flour
2 oz (50 g) caster sugar
1 large egg
2 oz (50 g) butter or margarine
4 tablespoon (½ cup) milk
Small amount of milk and demerara sugar to glaze

Put the fruit into a pie dish with the brown sugar and a little water.

Sift the flour and stir in the sugar.

Cut the fat into small pieces, and rub it into the flour mixture.

Make a well in the flour mixture.

Gradually beat in the egg and the milk and stir to make a dough.

Roll out the dough on a floured board to about ½ inch thick.

Cut into 8 rounds with a cutter.

Put the scones on top of the fruit.

Brush the tops with a little milk and sprinkle with demerara sugar.

Bake in a hot oven for 15 minutes, then reduce the temperature and bake for a further 20 minutes.

Oven: 400°F/200°C Gas Mark 6 for 15 minutes
Reduce to: 350°F/180°C Gas Mark 4 for 20 minutes

KENTISH CHERRY PANCAKES

Makes 8

4 oz (100 g) plain flour
1 large egg
½ pt (300 ml/ 1¼ cups) milk
A pinch of salt
Fat for frying
1 lb (450 g) stoned cherries, stewed lightly
2 oz (50 g) sugar
¼ pt (150 ml/ ⅔ cup) water
½ oz (15 g) cornflour
2 oz (50 g) raspberry jam
Cherry brandy to flavour
Whipped cream to decorate

Mix the sifted flour with the salt.

Make a well in the centre, drop in the egg, and beat to a smooth paste with a little of the milk.

Continue beating, gradually adding all the milk.

Melt the fat in a small shallow frying pan.

Pour into the hot fat enough batter to thinly cover the base of the pan.

When cooked on the underside, toss or turn and brown on the other side.

Fry 8 thin pancakes in this way.

Fill them with three quarters of the cooked cherries.

Roll up the pancakes and keep warm.

Reduce the sugar and water to a syrup by boiling.

Blend the cornflour with a little water.

Add the raspberry jam, and stir this mixture into the syrup.

Bring back to the boil.

Flavour with cherry brandy.

Simmer the sauce gently for 10 minutes.

Pour over the pancakes.

Decorate with whipped cream and the remaining cherries.

APPLE SNOW   Serves 4

1½ lbs (675 g) cooking apples
1 lemon
4 oz (100 g) caster sugar
2 large eggs
4 tablespoons (⅓ cup) water

Peel, core and cut the apples into quarters.

Squeeze the lemon.

Put the prepared apples and lemon juice in a saucepan with the water.

Cook very gently to a soft pulp.

When the apples are cold, strain off any juice.

Beat the sugar into the apple pulp, until smooth.

Separate the eggs.

Beat the whites until stiff and forming peaks.

Beat into the apple purée.

Pile the snow into one large or individual glass serving dishes.

Decorate with fresh or glacé fruit.

Serve with cream.

KENTISH FRUIT AND CREAM COMPOTE

Serves 3

8 oz (225 g) caster sugar
2 oz (50 g) stoned cherries
2 oz (50 g) red currants
4 oz (100 g) raspberries
4 oz (100 g) strawberries
½ pint (300 ml/ 1¼ cups) double cream

Put the cherries and red currants in a saucepan with the sugar.

Bring to the boil.

Simmer for 10 minutes, stirring continuously.

Add the strawberries and raspberries.

Simmer for a further 2 or 3 minutes, until all the fruit is soft.

Press the fruit through a sieve.

Leave to cool.

Stir in the cream.

Whisk the mixture quickly until it thickens.

Serve in individual dishes or glasses.

Chill before serving.

GOOSEBERRY OR FRESH FRUIT FOOL

Serves 4

Gooseberry Fool dates from the 15th century. Apricots, blackberries, plums, raspberries, rhubarb, or any kind of fresh fruit can be used to make the pulp in place of gooseberries.

1 lb (450 g) gooseberries
3 fl ozs (4½ tablespoons) water
4 oz (100 g) granulated sugar
½ pt (300 ml/ 1¼ cups) thick custard
¼ pt (150 ml/ ⅔ cup) double cream
Chopped nuts to decorate

Top and tail the gooseberries, or prepare the fruit according to type.

Simmer in the water and sugar until soft.

Pass the fruit through a sieve.

Leave the pulp to cool.

Make up the custard with milk and custard powder, and leave to cool.

Whip the cream lightly.

Mix the gooseberry pulp into the custard.

Fold in the cream.

Serve in individual dishes or glasses, decorated with the chopped nuts.

CHERRIES IN KIRSCH

Serves 4

1 lb (450 g) black cherries, stoned
2 oz (50 g) blanched almonds
½ pt (300 ml/ 1¼ cups) water
2 oz (50 g) granulated sugar
2 or 3 tablespoons Kirsch
Whipped double cream to decorate

Stuff the cherries with almonds to replace the stones.

Arrange a serving dish.

Boil the water with the sugar until it has reduced to a syrup.

Allow to cool.

Blend in the Kirsch.

Pour the syrup over the cherries.

Pipe the whipped cream on top.

Maraschino can be used in place of Kirsch.

CHERRIES IN RED WINE

Serves 4

1 lb (450 g) red cherries, stoned
¼ pt (150 ml/ ⅔ cup) red wine
4 oz (100 g) red currant jelly
A little arrowroot
Whipped double cream to decorate

Put the cherries in a saucepan with the wine. (This should be sufficient to just cover.)

Add the red currant jelly.

Simmer gently until the cherries are soft. (Do not allow them to break up).

Drain the fruit carefully, and return the juice to the pan.

Thicken with blended arrowroot.

Arrange the cherries in a serving dish.

Pour the thickened juice over the cherries.

Decorate with piped cream.

KENTISH HONEYED FRUIT SALAD

Serves 4

4 oz (100 g) red cherries
4 oz (100 g) raspberries preferably Malling Promise
4 oz (100 g) strawberries
4 oz (100 g) William pears
4 oz (100 g) Discovery (dessert) apples
2 tablespoons lemon juice
2 tablespoons Kentish honey
1 pint (600 ml/ 2½ cups) water

Stone the cherries.

Hull the raspberries and strawberries.

Peel and slice the pears.

Peel and slice the apples.

Sprinkle the apples with ½ the lemon juice to prevent browning.

Heat the water and honey together to make a syrup.

Add the sliced apples and pears and poach very gently over a low heat for a few minutes until soft.

Allow to cool.

Add the raspberries, strawberries and cherries.

Add 1 tablespoon of lemon juice and stir.

Put the fruit salad into a glass serving bowl.

Serve with pouring cream.

KENT APPLE AND CHEESE SCONE ROUND

Makes an 8 inch round

Scones are of very ancient origin. Before ovens were introduced, they were cooked on a griddle or 'bakestone'.

1 large cooking apple
12 oz (350 g) wholemeal flour
A little lemon juice
A pinch of salt
1 tablespoon baking powder
3 oz (75 g) butter or margarine
3 oz (75 g) caster sugar
¼ pt (150 ml/ ⅔ cup) milk (preferably sour), or enough to make a stiff dough
2 oz (50 g) grated cheese
A little extra milk

Peel, core and grate apple.

Sprinkle the grated apple with the lemon juice to prevent browning, and to add flavour.

Sieve flour, salt and baking powder together.

Rub in the butter or margarine until the mixture resembles fine breadcrumbs.

Stir in the caster sugar and grated apple.

Mix to a stiff dough with the milk.

On a floured board, roll out the dough to a round about ½ inch thick.

Brush the top with milk and sprinkle well with grated cheese.

Mark the round with a knife into 8 wedges.

Bake in a hot oven for 25 minutes or until golden brown.

Delicious served warm, and buttered in the middle.

Oven: 400°F/200°C Gas Mark 6

DOVER SPLITS

A 13th century chronicler described Dover as the 'Key to England'. It has seen great periods of invasion and defence, right up to the Second World War. In 55 BC Julius Caesar landed at Deal with 6,000 men. The Roman occupation was followed by invasion from Angles, Jutes and Saxons. Dover Castle was constructed mainly in the late 12th and 13th centuries, and dominates the town on a site which shows evidence of occupation or fortification since prehistoric times.

1 lb (450 g) plain flour
2 teaspoons baking powder
½ teaspoon salt
½ pt (150 ml/ ⅔ cup) milk
2 oz (50 g) lard
1 oz (25 g) butter or margarine
A little milk

Sift flour, baking powder and salt together.

Rub in the lard and butter.

Stir in the milk.

Mix to a stiff dough.

Roll out the dough on a floured board to ¾ inch thickness.

Cut into rounds with a cutter.

Brush tops of splits with milk.

Bake for 15 minutes in a hot oven.

Split in half and serve with butter, jam and thickly whipped cream.

Oven: 425°F/220°C Gas Mark 7

APPLE GINGERBREAD

Gingerbread has a long history in Britain. In early days it was made from a mixture of grated bread, ginger, liquorice, aniseed and pepper, sweetened with honey. This was made into a stiff paste with ale or claret, formed into flat cakes, often in the shape of men, letters or numbers, and then dried gently until hard and brittle.

2 oz (50 g) butter or margarine
2 oz (50 g) soft brown sugar
3 oz (75 g) black treacle or syrup
4 oz (100 g) plain flour
12 oz (350 g) cooking apples
1 teaspoon ground ginger
½ teaspoon bicarbonate of soda
½ teaspoon ground cloves
A little milk to mix

For the icing:
½ level teaspoon cinnamon
8 oz (225 g) icing sugar

Peel, core and chop the apples finely.

Line a greased, shallow 8 inch cake tin.

Melt the butter, sugar and syrup together over a gentle heat.

Remove from the heat, and blend in the sifted flour, ginger, bicarbonate of soda, and cloves.

Mix in the apples, then the milk to give a soft dropping consistency.

Spoon into the prepared cake tin and bake for 1 hour.

Allow the cake to cool.

Turn out and make sure it is completely cold before icing.

Mix the icing sugar with a little water and the cinnamon to a coating consistency.

Top the gingerbread with the icing glaze.

Oven: 350°F/180°C Gas Mark 4

KENTISH HUFFKINS

Huffkins are an East Kent tea bread. Traditionally they are thick flat cakes made of light bread with a hole in the middle, which can be filled with fruit, such as cherries or strawberries.

½ pt (300 ml/ 1¼ cups) milk
1 oz (25 g) sugar
1 oz (25 g) fresh yeast (or 1 tablespoon dried yeast)
1 lb (650 g) plain flour
1 teaspoon salt
2 oz (50 g) lard

Heat the milk until tepid.

Remove from the heat and stir in the sugar.

Crumble in the fresh yeast — or spinkle the dried yeast on top, and stand the liquid in a warm place until it becomes frothy, approximately 10 minutes.

Sieve the flour and salt together.

Rub in the fat until mixture resembles fine breadcrumbs.

Add the yeast liquid to the flour and mix to form a soft dough.

Knead lightly.

Cover the bowl with a cloth and put in a warm place for the dough to rise to double its size, approximately one hour.

Turn on to a floured board and knead again lightly.

Divide the dough into six pieces.

Roll each piece into a ball and flatten with the hand to make flat round cakes.

Place the cakes on a greased baking sheet.

Make a hole in the centre of each one by drawing the dough apart with two fingers of each hand or two wooden spoon handles.

Sprinkle the cakes with flour.

Put the cakes on the baking sheet in a warm place to rise for a further 30 minutes.

Bake in a hot oven for 20 minutes until golden brown.

Remove from oven, and to keep the crusts soft, wrap in a cloth until cool.

Oven: 425°F/220°C Gas Mark 7

TUNBRIDGE WELLS CAKES   Makes 12

8 oz (225 g) plain flour
4 oz (100 g) caster sugar
2 oz (50 g) butter or margarine
2 oz (50 g) caraway seeds
A little milk to mix

Sift the flour.

Rub in the butter or margarine until the mixture resembles fine breadcrumbs.

Add the sugar and caraway seeds.

Mix to a stiff dough with the milk.

Knead thoroughly.

Roll out thinly.

Cut into 1½ inch rounds with a biscuit cutter.

Put on a greased backing sheet and prick with a fork.

Bake for 30 minutes.

Oven: 325°F/160°C Gas Mark 3

BRANDY SNAPS

In old recipe books, these rolled biscuits were called Jumbals, and sometimes flavoured with carraway seeds or mace.

4 oz (100 g) self-raising flour
1 small teaspoon ground ginger
4 oz (100 g) unsalted butter or margarine
4 oz (100 g) golden syrup or black treacle
4 oz (100 g) brown sugar
A little grated lemon rind
½ pt (300 ml/ 1½ cups) whipped double cream to fill
Brandy to flavour cream, if liked

Sieve the flour and ground ginger together.

Add the grated lemon rind to the flour.

Melt the fat in a saucepan over a low heat.

Remove from the heat.

Stir in the flour, syrup and sugar, mixing well together.

Grease a flat baking tray or trays.

Spoon the mixture onto the tray in small amounts.

Flatten with the hand or a palette knife.

Allow plenty of room for each biscuit to spread to about double its size.

Bake in a hot oven for about 10 minutes, or until flat, brown and bubbling.

Remove from the oven.

After about a minute or as soon as it can be done without breaking, ease the biscuits from the tin with a knife.

Curl each biscuit tightly round the greased handle of a wooden spoon.

The biscuits will harden quite quickly, and can be slipped off the handle.

Fill with cream before serving. If liked the cream can be flavoured with a few drops of brandy.

Brandy snaps are best eaten shortly after cooking, as after a few hours they go soft, unless kept in an airtight tin.

The mixture can be prepared in advance and stored in an airtight container in the refrigerator before cooking, if desired.

Oven: 400°F/200°C Gas Mark 6

LAURA'S ALMOND MACAROON BISCUITS

Makes 12

2 egg whites
6 oz (175 g) caster sugar
5 oz (150 g) ground almonds
2 teaspoons lemon juice
¼ teaspoon almond essence
Rice paper

Separate the eggs.

Beat the whites until stiff.

Fold in 5 oz of the sugar, ground almonds, lemon juice and almond essence.

Line a baking sheet with rice paper.

Spoon the mixture on to the paper in small mounds well apart.

Shape into flat rounds.

Sprinkle with the rest of the caster sugar.

Bake in the oven for 25 minutes or until golden.

When the biscuits are nearly cold, remove them from the baking tin and cut or tear round the rice paper.

Oven: 350°F/180°C Gas Mark 4

GRAN'S BOILED CAKE

12 oz (350 g) mixed fruit
4 oz (100 g) brown sugar
4 oz (100 g) margarine or butter
¼ pt (150 ml/ ⅔ cup) water
1 egg
8 oz (225 g) self-raising flour, sieved

Put the fruit, sugar, fat and water in a saucepan.

Bring slowly to simmering point.

Simmer gently for 20 minutes.

Allow mixture to cool.

Beat the egg thoroughly.

Stir into the mixture.

Stir the sieved flour into the mixture to give a dropping consistency.

Put the mixture into a greased 6 inch cake tin.

Bake in a very moderate oven for about 1½ hours.

Oven: 325°F/160°C Gas Mark 3

KENTISH CAKE

4 oz (100 g) butter or margarine
4 oz (100 g) caster sugar
4 oz (100 g) self-raising flour
3 small eggs or 2 large eggs (separated)
1 oz (25 g) desiccated coconut
2 oz (50 g) cocoa powder
1 oz (25 g) ground almonds
A little vanilla essence

Cream the butter and sugar.

Beat in the egg yolks.

Fold in the flour, coconut, cocoa, almonds and vanilla essence to taste.

Whisk the egg whites until stiff.

Fold into the mixture.

Spoon into a lined, greased 6 inch round cake tin.

Bake for 25 minutes.

Oven: 375°F/190°C Gas Mark 5

KENTISH FLEAD CAKES

These were thin rounds of flead pastry brushed with beaten egg, and baked until golden brown.

Flead is the inner membrane of pig's intestine. It is a fine skin, full of particles of pure lard. It was rubbed into flour to make the flead pastry, as lard or margarine would be used today.

MOTHER'S ROCK CAKES

Makes 12

8 oz (225 g) self-raising flour
A pinch of salt
4 oz (100 g) margarine or butter
2 oz (50 g) granulated sugar
4 oz (100 g) currants or sultanas
1 oz (25 g) chopped mixed peel, if liked
1 egg
Milk to mix, if required
A little caster sugar for dusting

Sieve the flour and salt together.

Stir in the sugar and the washed fruit.

Beat the egg.

Stir the egg into the mixture.

The consistency should be fairly stiff — only add a little milk to mix if necessary.

Put teaspoons of the mixture into rough blobs on to a greased baking sheet. (Do not smooth. It is the irregularity of shape that gives rise to the name, and that is also why it is important for the mixture to be stiff and hold its shape).

Bake in a moderately hot oven for 15 minutes until golden brown.

Dust the cakes with caster sugar while still warm.

Oven: 400°F/200°C Gas Mark 6

OAST CAKES

These cakes were traditionally eaten at a Kentish hop feast, which was known as a 'hopkin'.

They were also cooked by the women in the Kentish hop gardens on iron plates over emergency stoves to eat with cheese and some beer as a snack during the short morning break from hop picking. Sometimes they were eaten at tea time dredged with vanilla or cinnamon flavoured sugar. An old Kentish recipe suggests the dough is mixed with half and half parsnip wine and water.

8 oz (225 g) self-raising flour
2 oz (50 g) margarine or lard
2 oz (50 g) caster sugar
3 oz (75 g) currants
A pinch of salt
Fat for frying
A little water

Sift the flour with the salt.

Rub in the margarine or lard until the mixture resembles fine breadcrumbs.

Add the sugar and currants.

Mix to a light dough with the water.

Roll out and cut into rounds with a ½ inch biscuit cutter.

Fry in shallow fat, turning once, until golden brown.

Serve hot.

RED WINE SAUCE
Serves 6

½ pt (300 ml/ 1¼ cups) port wine
¼ pt (150 ml/ ⅔ cup) cherry juice
¼ pt (150 ml/ ⅔ cup) water
2 oz (50 g) cornflour

Put the port wine and cherry juice into a saucepan and bring to the boil.

Add the water.

Mix the cornflour to a smooth cream with a little of the liquid.

Add the cornflour cream to the sauce and bring back to the boil, stirring continuously.

Cook a few minutes, still stirring, until the sauce thickens.

APPLE SAUCE
Serves 4

A traditionally accompaniment to pork and an aid to digestion.

4 large Bramley cooking apples
Water for cooking
1 teaspoon sugar
1 teaspoon lemon juice
1 oz (25 g) butter or margarine

Peel, core and slice the apples.

Put the apple slices in a saucepan with sufficient water to just moisten.

Simmer very gently until reduced to a pulp.

Stir in the sugar and lemon juice.

Beat in the butter with a wooden spoon until the sauce is smooth. Serve cold.

CAPER SAUCE

An ideal sauce to serve with boiled or roast lamb. If made with fish stock instead of meat, caper sauce is excellent with fish.

1 oz (25 g) margarine or butter
1 oz (25 g) plain flour
½ pt (300 ml/ 1¼ cups) meat or fish stock
1 oz (25 g) capers
2 tablespoons white wine vinegar
Salt and pepper

Melt the fat in a saucepan.

Add the flour.

Stir to make a roux, and cook over a low heat for a few minutes, still stirring.

Gradually add the stock.

Bring to the boil and continue to stir, until the sauce thickens, for about 3 minutes.

Season to taste.

Add the capers, either left whole or chopped as preferred.

Stir in the vinegar.

Simmer for a further 2 minutes.

Serve in a sauce boat.

PICKLED KENTISH CHERRIES

Because of the vinegar, use an alluminium, stainless steel or enamelled saucepan, and not a brass, copper or iron one, when making pickles and chutneys. Also use a wooden spoon for mixing.

4 lbs (1.75 kg) black cherries
2 pt (1.15 litres/ 5 cups) malt vinegar
2 lb (900 g) granulated sugar
½ oz (15 g) cloves
1 teaspoon allspice
1 teaspoon ground nutmeg
1 teaspoon powdered cinnamon

Stone the cherries.

Put them in a saucepan with the vinegar, sugar, cloves, allspice, nutmeg and cinnamon and bring to the boil.

Simmer gently for a few minutes, until the sugar is dissolved and the cherries soft.

Remove from the heat, cover the saucepan, and leave to stand for 2 hours.

Carefully remove the fruit and pack them into sterilised jars within 1 inch of the top.

Pour the sweet vinegar liquid over the fruit stopping ½ inch from the top.

To avoid the vinegar evaporating, cover with a metal lid with a vinegar-proof lining or greaseproof paper covered with muslin dipped in melted fat, or candle wax. Tie down.

Store the pickled cherries in a dark, cool and dry place.

Allow to mature for 3 months before using.

Serve with hot or cold meat, also excellent with curry.

DAMSON CHEESE

Fruit cheeses were made when there was a glut of fruit, as they are not a very economical way of using fruit — but delicious.

6 lbs (2.75 kg) damsons, fully ripe
3 lbs (1.4 kg) granulated sugar
2 pints (1.15 litres/ 4 cups) water
A little brandy or port

Stone the damsons.

Blanch about 24 of the kernels in boiling water, and then crush them.

Put the damsons and water into a preserving pan, and cook gently until the fruit is soft.

Rub through a sieve.

Put the damson purée and the sugar back into the preserving pan and cook gently, stirring all the time until the sugar dissolves.

Then boil gently, stirring to prevent sticking, until the preserve forms into a thick paste.

Stir in the crushed kernels.

A little brandy or port may be added to the preserve.

Cook slightly, but while still hot pour into a small, dry, warm, sterilised jars.

A tip to prevent sticking is to grease the bottom of the preserving pan with butter.

Damson cheese is excellent served sliced and decorated with split almonds, with a glass of port wine.

SARAH'S MARMALADE   Makes 6 lbs (2.75 kg)

This method of making marmalade uses fruit whole. As less sugar is added than usual, the marmalade tastes deliciously fruity. The oranges may be cooked from frozen. This allows the fruit to be bought in season, stored in the freezer and the marmalade to be made at any time of year.

2 lb (1 kg) Seville oranges
1 lemon
1 sweet orange
3½ lbs (1.6 kg) preserving or granulated sugar
4 (2.25 litres/10 cups) — 5 pints (3 litres/13 cups) water

Wash the fruit.

Cut out the core from the top of each orange.

Put the fruit in a preserving dish.

Add sufficient water to allow the fruit to float — approximately 4 (2.25 litres/10 cups) — 5 pints (3 litres/13 cups).

Bring to the boil and simmer until the orange skins are soft.

Remove the oranges one by one.

Cut the fruit in half and remove the pips.

Cut the fruit into shreds with a knife or electric shredder.

Put the shredded fruit back into the pan.

Add the sugar.

Bring the mixture to simmering point stirring constantly until the sugar is dissolved.

Bring to a rapid boil.

Continue boiling for about 15 minutes until the marmalade begins to set.

To test for setting point — spoon a little marmalade on to a cool saucer.

Push the marmalade gently with the little finger, and if it wrinkles it is set.

If not, continue boiling and test again every 10-15 minutes.

When cooked allow the marmalade to cool.

Pour into clean 1 lb jam jars and cover tightly with purchased jam covers.

KENTISH CHERRY AND RASPBERRY JAM
Makes about 5 lbs (2.25 kg)

In Victorian times housewives preferred the name preserve or conserve, to jam. The word 'jam' was considered rather vulgar. Cherry jam was a famous speciality on Kentish farms.

To prevent jam from sticking and forming too much scum, grease the bottom of the preserving pan with butter. Should a lot of scum form during cooking, drop in a knob of butter.

2 lbs (1 kg) Morello cherries
4 lbs (1.75 kg) raspberries
5 lbs (2.25 kg) preserving sugar
3 tablespoons (¼ cup) lemon juice

Stone the cherries.

Put them in a preserving pan with the raspberries and lemon juice.

Bring to the boil and simmer for 15 minutes.

Remove from the heat and take off any scum with a spoon.

Add the sugar.

Simmer until all the sugar is dissolved, then increase the heat to bring the jam to a rolling boil.

Boil rapidly, stirring frequently until the jam hangs on the spoon, or a little will set on a cold plate.

When cooled, pour into hot sterilised jars and cover tightly with purchased jam covers.

GREEN TOMATO AND APPLE CHUTNEY

2 lbs (1 kg) green tomatoes
2 lb (1 kg) cooking apples
1 lb (450 g) shallots or onions
6 red chillies
2 oz (50 g) garlic
12 oz (350 g) sultanas
½ oz (15 g) ground ginger
8 oz (225 g) demerara sugar
1 pint (600 ml/, 2½ cups) malt vinegar

Peel the tomatoes by plunging them into hot water for a moment or two.

Cut the tomatoes into quarters.

Peel and core the apples, and slice.

Peel and slice the shallots or onions.

Mix the vegetables together.

Put into a saucepan.

Chop the garlic finely.

Add the sugar, chillies, sultanas, garlic, ginger and vinegar.

Bring to the boil.

Simmer for about 1½ hours until thick, soft and brown, stirring frequently.

Pour the mixture into sterilised dry jars.

Cover with purchased jam covers, then with a round cloth, brushed with melted candle grease, to make an air-tight seal.

Serve as an accompaniment to cold meat, cheese or curry.

HOP BEER

Makes about 20 pints

3 oz (75 g) hops
3 gallons (13.5 litres/ 24 pints) water
1¼ lb (575 g) brown sugar
3 level tablespoons (¼ cup) yeast

Add the hops to the water in a large saucepan.

Boil together for 45 minutes.

Add the sugar, and stir until dissolved.

Strain the liquid into a big bowl.

Leave until lukewarm.

Take 1 teacupful of the liquid from the bowl.

Add the yeast to the teacup. Stir.

Return the contents of the teacup to the big bowl, and stir well.

Cover the bowl with a thick cloth.

Leave for 48 hours.

Skim off the froth.

Strain into clean bottles and cork securely.

Leave for 6 days before using.

PARSNIP WINE

Makes about 7 pints (4 litres)

3 lbs (1.5 g) parsnips
1 lemon
1 orange
8 pints (4.5 litres/ 1 gallon) water
3 lbs (1.5 g) loaf sugar
1 tablespoon yeast
Piece of toast

Peel the parsnips.

Cut them into pieces about ½ inch thick.

Grate the rind of the orange and lemon and cut up the flesh.

Put the parsnips, grated rind and fruit into the water in a large pan.

Boil until the parsnips are tender.

Strain the liquid.

Then add the sugar.

Return the liquid to the heat and stir until all the sugar is dissolved.

Simmer the liquid for 45 minutes.

Put the liquid in a large earthenware container.

Spread the yeast onto the toast.

Put the toast in the liquid.

Leave the container in a warm place, such as an airing cupboard, for 10 days.

Stir well each day, reaching right to the bottom of the container.

Strain.

Return to the large earthenware container.

Do not fill or cover, as the liquid will ferment and rise up.

When the wine has stopped fermenting, pour it into sterilised bottles and cork tightly.

Strain and bottle again in six months.

Best kept for six further months before drinking.

MULLED ALE   Makes 36 wine glasses

4 pints (2.25 litres/ 10 cups) ale
½ pint (300 ml/ 1 ¼ cups) rum
2 pints (1.15 litres/ 5 cups) water
10 oz (275 g) granulated sugar
½ teaspoon nutmeg
½ teaspoon cinnamon
½ teaspoon ground cloves
2 lemons

Put the ale, rum and water into a large saucepan.

Add the sugar, nutmeg, cinnamon and ground cloves.

Heat gently, stirring occasionally, until all the sugar is dissolved.

Increase the heat gently, until the mixture is almost boiling.

Cut the lemons into slices, discarding the pips.

Serve hot with the lemon slices, preferably in a punch bowl.

TO BREW MARGATE ALE

Margate is known as Blackpool in Kent. The first bathing machines were used here in the middle of the 18th century. In those days the town was affectionately nicknamed 'Bartholomew Fair by the Sea'.

The Blessing of the Sea takes place at this busy resort and port annually in January and at Whitstable in July. This recipe is an original held in the Kent Archives.

Take 9 Strikes* of Malt for half a Hogs head* of Ale, make the water just ready to boil (but do not boil it) then mash it thick, covering it up close, with some dry malt strewed over 16 Times. Let it stand for 4 hours then let it off gently dashing in by degrees 4 Gallons of cold water on the malt, when you have got as much wort* as will fill your half Hogshead allowing for waste in boiling throw in by a great dish full of warm water at a time, for the small ale or beer till you have as much as will fill half a Hogshead of small ale or a Hogshead of Beer.

    Boil your strong wort two Hours and a half with 3 pounds of good Hops well rubbed in, if the Hops are not very good allow half a Pound more. When this wort is boiled the Time mentioned put it into the Cooler, thro' a Sieve. When cold enough let it be run into the working tub, and when milk warm pour gently your barm* on it, when it works beat it in every hour gently, but not to the bottom. When you have done this 3 or 4 Times, beat it well to the bottom once in 2 hours for 3 or 4 Times and then let it stand till the Barm falls before you tun it, scum the Barm cleen off keep it covered all the Time it works. Stop the Vessel up the day after it is tunned. The same hops will serve for the other Drink.

    October is the best Time to brew this in. Keep this five or six months before you bottle it.

Strike — a denomination of dry measure varying between half a bushel and two or four bushels.
Hogshead — a large cask for liquids.
Wort — infusion of malt or other grain which after fermentation becomes beer.
Barm — froth that forms on the top of fermenting liquors.